GYMNASTICS

Gymnastics coaches
Linda Wallenberg Bragg
and Scott Gay and the
following athletes were
photographed for this
book:
    Jill Ames,
    Tony Aretz,
    Nikki Benedict,
    Kristy Bowman,
    Matt Bulger,
    Heidi Cady,
    Sara Dunphy,
    R.J. Emery,
    Beth Flaherty,
    Andrew Gagner,
    Andrew Hackman,
    Christian Hyun,
    Nicholas Johnson,
    Lori Lehman,
    Pat Nelson,
    Adam Reichow,
    Cathy Sohn,
    Stacy Swigart,
    Mark Tundel,
    Kelli Ueland.

LERNER
SPORTS
A DIVISION OF LERNER PUBLISHING GROUP

PLAY BY PLAY

GYMNASTICS

Linda
Wallenberg
Bragg

Photographs by
Andy King

Lerner Publications Company ● Minneapolis

Copyright © 2000 by Lerner Publications Company

Photo Acknowledgments

Photographs are reproduced with the permission of: p. 7, Scala/Art Resource, N.Y.; p. 8, The Bettmann Archive; p. 9 (top), UPI/Bettmann; p. 9 (bottom), ALLSPORT/Steve Powell; p. 10, ALLSPORT; p. 11, ALLSPORT/Doug Pensinger; p. 14, ALLSPORT/Tony Duffy; p. 63, ALLSPORT/Chris Cole; p. 74 (top), ALLSPORT/Gary M. Prior.

Library of Congress Cataloging-in-Publication Data

Bragg, Linda Wallenberg.
    Play-by-play gymnastics / Linda Wallenberg Bragg ; photographs by Andy King.
        p. cm.
        Rev. ed. of: Fundamental gymnastics. ©1995
        Includes bibliographical references.
        Summary: Provides information about participating in gymnastics, including the history, equipment, skills, and practice necessary.
        ISBN 0–8225-9877-9 (pbk. : alk. paper)
        1. Gymnastics—Juvenile literature. [1. Gymnastics.]
    I. King, Andy, ill. II. Title.
    GV461.3.B72   2000
    796.44—dc21   99–056745

Manufactured in the United States of America
1 2 3 4 5 6 – JP – 05 04 03 02 01 00

Contents

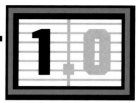

HOW THIS SPORT GOT STARTED

Imagine tiptoeing on a 4-inch wide piece of wood. In less than one second, you lift your arms and propel your body upward into a tight little tucked ball. For a split second you see the ceiling. Now—quick!—you squeeze your ankles tight. In a flash, that skinny piece of wood is under your feet again. You did it! You landed safely—on the **balance beam.**

Such is the life of a gymnast. Gymnasts perform physical activities that require strength, balance, and body control. If this excitement appeals to you, you're probably one of thousands of young people, girls and boys, all over the world, who have fallen in love with this dynamic and challenging sport.

Gymnasts were featured in some ancient Greek artworks, such as this vase.

7

Friedrich Jahn formed the first club for gymnastics in 1811 in Germany.

Gymnastics combines the thrill of turning your body upside down with the artistry of dancing. A gymnast tries to perform every maneuver to absolute perfection. Because of its grace and beauty, some people consider gymnastics a performing art rather than a sport.

Plato, a Greek philosopher, said:

> *God, I should say,*
> *has given men two arts,*
> *music and gymnastics.*

Plato believed that music educated the mind and gymnastics trained the body.

THE HISTORY OF GYMNASTICS

We don't know exactly how or why people started doing gymnastics but there are pictures of athletes jumping, running, climbing ropes, and tumbling on ancient Greek vases. The Greeks included gymnastics in their Olympic Games, which began more than 2,000 years ago. Their word "gymnastics" was used for any physical activity that was performed in a training center called a gymnasium.

Friedrich Jahn from Germany is known as the father of gymnastics. In 1811 he built an outdoor gymnastics center and used crude equipment to teach students gymnastics moves. His was the first gymnastics club, and

Left, Mitsuo Tsukahara of Japan was famous throughout the world when he competed during the 1970s. Below, Bart Conner's clean technique helped the United States team win the gold medal at the 1984 Olympic Games.

clubs are still very important in training young gymnasts.

Between 1850 and 1900, gymnastics became popular all over. Gymnastics was one of nine original sports in the first modern Olympics, held in Athens, Greece, in 1896. Only men competed in those Olympics. They performed on six pieces of equipment, called **apparatus:** the **parallel bars, horizontal bar, rings, pommel horse, vault,** and ropes. (They competed in rope climbing instead of the **floor exercise.**) The Olympic Games encouraged people who were interested in gymnastics competition to

Watching the dynamic and personable Olga Korbut of the Soviet Union compete in the 1972 Olympic Games inspired youngsters all over the world to learn how to compete in gymnastics.

develop rules, equipment standards, and regulations.

At first, girls weren't encouraged to take part in gymnastics. Some people didn't think women had the physical strength and power for such a sport. However, women's gymnastics team competition was introduced in the 1928 Olympics. At the Olympic Games in 1952, the female gymnasts from the Soviet Union dazzled the crowd. Soon, special equipment was developed for events that only women competed in. Individual competition in women's gymnastics began and quickly became popular.

When the 1960 Olympics were broadcast on television, many people were dazzled by the beauty of women's gymnastics. By the 1970s, there were more famous female gymnasts than male. As the sport's popularity increased, athletes from many countries vied for Olympic honors. By the 1990s, gymnasts from the United States were among those at the top.

This book will introduce you to the basics of the sport of gymnastics. Just like any other sport, gymnastics requires you to train your body. But it also requires you to train your mind and your emotions.

Dominique Dawes burst onto the American gymnastics scene in the 1990s. She was a member of the U.S. Olympic team that won a gold medal in the 1996 Olympics.

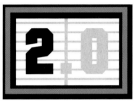

BASICS

Anyone can learn to do gymnastics moves but it takes many years for someone to develop into a competitive gymnast. That's why the best gymnasts usually started taking gymnastics lessons when they were three to five years old.

In the beginning lessons, the coach mainly works on developing a gymnast's coordination, balance, and flexibility. Many young children are either naturally strong or naturally flexible. The best gymnasts are both.

Toddlers work on pointing their toes and stretching their muscles. They will even start tumbling.

By the time beginning gymnasts start school, they are usually working on gymnastics apparatus and developing strength in specific muscles. A lot of time is spent learning tumbling skills but the apparatus events are becoming the big challenge.

WHAT TO WEAR?

Gymnasts, both male and female, follow specific rules about what to wear when competing. If a gymnast doesn't dress properly for competition, he or she will lose some points (called a deduction).

Although boys are no longer required to wear white pants when performing on pommel horse, parallel bars, horizontal bar, and rings, many still do. For vault and floor exercise, they wear shorts.

Most coaches have rules about what gymnasts should wear when practicing. When a coach is physically assisting (spotting) a gymnast, the clothing must not hinder the coach. That's why most coaches don't allow T-shirts and require that long hair be tied back. Some gymnasts wear gymnastic slippers, and others prefer to perform in their bare feet.

Nadia Comaneci competed for Romania in the Olympics during the 1970s.

WHAT'S IN A NAME?

Part of a gymnast's score is for originality. Original routines get higher scores. Skills are usually named after the gymnast who first performs them.

For example, the **tsukahara** vault is named after a Japanese gymnast, Mitsuo Tsukahara, who competed in the 1970s. The **comaneci** dismount on the uneven parallel bars is named after legendary Romanian gymnast Nadia Comaneci, who stunned the world in the 1970s with her amazing string of perfect routines.

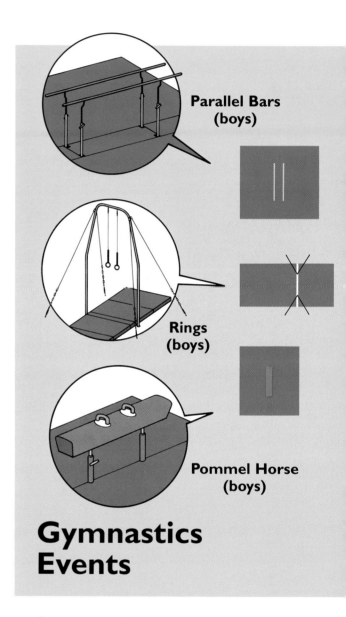

Parallel Bars (boys)

Rings (boys)

Pommel Horse (boys)

Gymnastics Events

There are six events in boys' gymnastics: floor exercise, vault, pommel horse, rings, parallel bars, and horizontal bar. Girls compete in four events: floor exercise, vault, **uneven parallel bars,** and balance beam.

Boys and girls both compete on the floor exercise mat, but the boys' floor routine emphasizes tumbling and isn't performed to music. Girls' floor

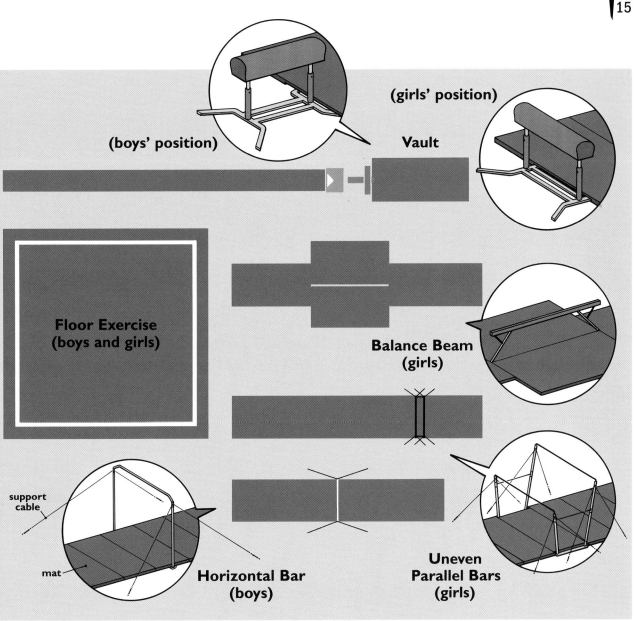

(boys' position)

(girls' position)

Vault

Floor Exercise (boys and girls)

Balance Beam (girls)

support cable

mat

Horizontal Bar (boys)

Uneven Parallel Bars (girls)

routines are performed to music and include dance moves.

Boys and girls both compete on the vault. However, the girls vault over the horse with it s*ideways* while the boys vault over the horse *lengthwise*.

For boys, the bars are side by side, or parallel. Girls compete on the uneven parallel bars—one bar is higher than the other.

Although the boys' events have no direct counterpart to the girls' balance beam, many people believe the beam is similar to the pommel horse. Both of these events present a great challenge to the gymnast just to stay on the apparatus. For many gymnasts, these events require much longer practice periods to perfect than do the others.

BOYS' EVENTS

In floor exercise, a gymnast has a standard number of seconds in which to perform sequences of tumbling skills, called a routine. The routine must show strength, timing, control, dynamic power, and precision.

In the photographs on this page and the next, Mark is shown doing a basic floor exercise skill called a **front handspring.** This skill requires him to spring forward and upward into the air with his body slightly arched and leaning forward.

Mark starts from a stretched stand. He takes a quick run and then places his hands shoulder-width apart on the floor. He kicks his rear leg into the air and then extends his front leg. His

shoulders **block** as his hips pass through the upside-down position. This causes his body to rise. The landing can be on one foot and then the other foot, or on both feet together.

Men used to perform their floor exercise routines on bare floors or on strips of mats with very little padding. Modern floor exercise equipment is more sophisticated. For most

competition and advanced training, the floor consists of either foam blocks or springs mounted under at least one layer of wood. Another layer of thick foam is placed on top of the wood, with a piece of carpet measuring 40 feet by 40 feet on top of the foam. This type of floor, called a rebound or **spring floor,** helps protect the gymnast from injury.

The vault is also called the horse. Boys use it positioned lengthwise. The vault is a padded wooden structure 3 feet, 7 inches high. The routine the gymnast performs over a vault is also called a vault, and it takes just four or five seconds to complete.

A springboard is placed in front of the vault. When training, gymnasts often use a mini-trampoline instead of a springboard. In the photographs on this page and the next, Christian is using a mini-tramp.

Christian begins somewhere near the end of the long cushioned runway. First, he takes an explosive run

and pushes off the mini-trampoline. **Preflight** is the term for the entry onto the vault itself. The gymnast should only touch the horse for a fraction of a second before thrusting off it. Next comes the **postflight,** which usually includes a flip or a **twist** or both. Then Christian does a controlled landing onto protective landing mats on the other side of the vault.

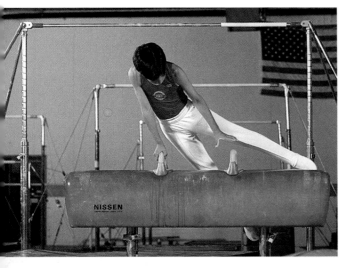

The pommel horse, or side horse, is a padded structure that has two handles on it called pommels. The pommel horse is 3 feet, 7 inches high. The gymnast supports his weight on the pommels while swinging from side to side and forward and back. The gymnast grasps and regrasps the pommels to allow his legs to pass beneath his hands.

Christian, at left, is beginning to learn how to move on the pommel horse. Young gymnasts such as Andrew, below, often begin to learn pommel horse moves on a piece of training equipment called a mushroom. Andrew is practicing his **circles** on the mushroom. Eventually he will use this skill on the pommel horse.

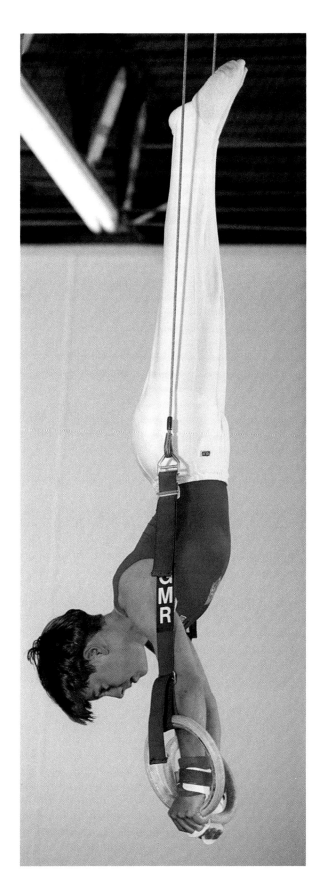

The still rings (rings for short) are completely circular, made of wood or fiberglass, and hang by straps from a steel frame. The rings are about 1 foot, 7½ inches apart and hang about 8 feet, 3 inches above the ground. The gymnast does circle and swinging movements. He also stops occasionally to show control, as Pat is doing in his handstand at left. The gymnast is also expected to show strength, as Nick is doing below with a back lever.

The parallel bars are two wooden or fiberglass bars, 11½ feet long and about 1½ feet apart. They are supported on **uprights** mounted on a single steel base. The bars are 5½ feet above the ground. Most of the gymnast's movements are done above the bars. The gymnast keeps his routine flowing. Above, Tony is showing good swing technique.

Perhaps the most thrilling of the boys' events is the horizontal bar, or high bar. This is an 8-foot long steel bar placed about 8 feet above the floor. The bar must be high enough to allow the gymnast to swing all the way around it with circling movements. The high bar is often lowered for beginning gymnasts who are just getting used to its height.

At right, Christian is demonstrating the basic swing used in high bar work. It's called a **giant swing.** When doing a giant, the gymnast holds onto the bar with both hands circling around the bar. Christian extends and then tightens his body during this maneuver.

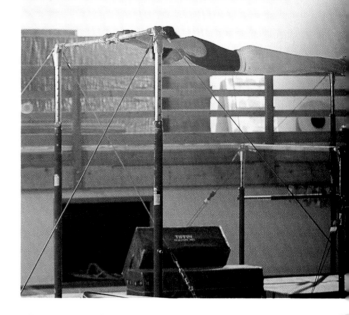

GIRLS' EVENTS

In the floor exercise routine, a gymnast must use good technique with pointed toes and a near-perfect body line. Sara illustrates this attention to detail in her **front walkover.**

The floor exercise routine needs a balance of tumbling and dance, and must be choreographed to music. The entire routine must be completed within a 1½-minute time limit.

A floor exercise routine requires a great deal of endurance. The last **tumbling pass** should be as difficult and exciting as the first.

The girls' vault event is similar to the boys' except that the vault is turned sideways rather than lengthwise. The vaulting apparatus, or horse, is 3 feet, 7 inches high. Girls and boys do basically the same vaults.

Stacy is demonstrating a vault on these two pages. After she sprints down the runway, she hits the board, enters the preflight phase, and pushes off the horse.

Stacy twists on the postflight. She tries to **stick** the landing, which means landing without taking any steps to regain her balance.

Heidi injured her knee but after it healed, she began doing gymnastics again. She wears a brace to protect her knee from injury.

The uneven parallel bars (or asymmetric bars) are two bars slotted into two sets of steel uprights. Each bar is the same length as the boys' horizontal bar. One bar is 7 feet, 6 inches above the floor and the other is 4 feet, 11 inches.

Some people think that the uneven parallel bars are the most dynamic of all the girls' events, combining the skill of the parallel bars with the thrill of the horizontal bar. In recent years,

many of the skills that were once thought only possible on the high bar are being performed on the uneven parallel bars.

A gymnast on the uneven parallel bars moves in a continuous flow of swinging and circling. Heidi demonstrates this with her giant swing.

A balance beam may be made of wood or aluminum. The beam is usually padded, with a suede covering. It is 4 inches wide and 16 feet, 5 inches long. The beam is set 3 feet, 11 inches above the floor for competition. It may be set lower for practice. The gymnast's balance beam routine can't take longer than 1 minute and 30 seconds. Timing begins at the moment the gymnast's feet leave the floor in a **mount.** A **dismount** completes her routine.

The balance beam is used to demonstrate balance and poses. Sara, at left, is showing precision and balance in this **handstand.** The gymnast must also dance on the beam. And the gymnast must also do a series of tumbling skills, such as the back walkover Jill is doing below.

BUILDING BLOCKS

Learning to do gymnastics is like climbing a ladder. Each skill should build on the last—just like climbing up a ladder one rung at a time.

Some gymnasts progress faster than others. Just as some people can reach the top of a ladder by skipping rungs, some gymnasts can skip steps in the learning process. But every gymnast must understand several key principles.

First, gymnasts must learn body awareness. A gymnast must know exactly where he or she is in the air while performing an aerial maneuver. A gymnast also must understand body alignment. A body flips and twists more cleanly and safely if every part of the body is in line. Knowing the correct alignment for each skill helps keep a gymnast safe.

Also, gymnasts must be prepared for falls. Falling is inevitable while a person is learning skills. Knowing how to recover from a fall and how to perform a proper dismount landing are essential parts of doing gymnastics. Gymnasts practice skills that help them land safely.

OTHER EQUIPMENT

In addition to the apparatus, gymnasts need equipment to make their routines comfortable and safe.

Most gymnasts use chalk (actually magnesium carbonate) on their hands and sometimes their feet to ensure a good grip on the apparatus. The chalk helps keep hands and feet from getting sweaty. Sometimes coaches and gymnasts put the chalk directly on the apparatus.

Many gymnasts also use **grips,** or hand-guards, when working on the rings or the various types of bars. There is a lot of friction between the palms of the gymnast's hands and the apparatus. Without grips, the gymnast's hands might blister or tear.

Landing mats are absolutely necessary. These mats are 4 to 10 inches high and often have a 1-inch base mat underneath for further protection. Landing mats are used to cushion and protect the gymnast when he or she is doing a dismount.

Coaches and gymnasts should check the apparatus often to be sure the equipment is stable and correctly set up. Safety is everyone's business.

One basic gymnastics concept is that a gymnast's body moves best in the air when it's in one of three positions: **tuck, pike,** or **layout.**

When Stacy's knees are tucked in close so that her body resembles a ball, she will rotate faster than if her body is stretched out. A coach usually teaches the tuck position to gymnasts who are learning to flip in the air.

As gymnasts advance, they learn to straighten out their legs and perform in a pike or layout position. In a pike position, the gymnast bends at the hips but keeps his or her legs straight.

In a layout position, the gymnast's entire body is in a straight line. In these positions, the body moves more slowly through the air. Many people feel these positions are more pleasing to watch than the tucked position.

Once you have learned the layout position, your coach may teach you to twist your body either half or all the way around as you do a maneuver. With that move, you're on your way!

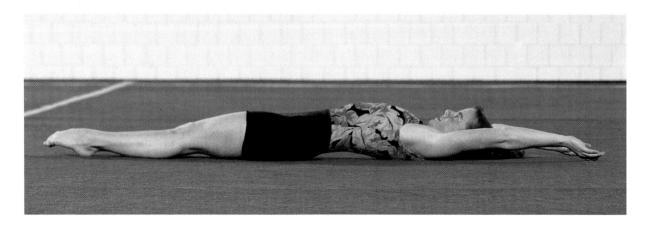

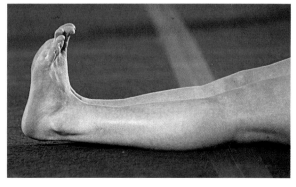

Gymnasts especially need flexible legs, backs, and shoulders. The **pancake** Adam is doing shows his leg and back flexibility. Although some gymnasts are born more flexible than others, all gymnasts must constantly work on maintaining or increasing their flexibility. Even ankle flexibility is important. In gymnastics, stretched ankles and pointed toes look better than flexed ankles.

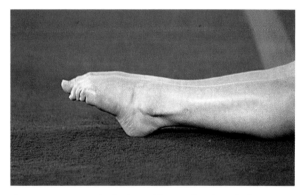

Gymnasts stretch their ankles and point their toes to achieve a clean line in their performances.

Flexing your ankles breaks the pleasing body line and isn't considered to be good technique.

Not only should gymnasts be flexible, they must also be very strong. Events such as the uneven parallel bars for girls and the still rings for boys demand strength.

Most gymnasts build their strength by doing conditioning workouts. Sometimes practicing the basic skills of gymnastics is part of the conditioning sessions, but gymnasts also do specific exercises that help them develop strength in different parts of their bodies.

For example, Matt's **straddle** hold, left, shows strength in his arms, legs, and abdomen. Gymnasts sometimes do **V-ups** instead of regular sit-ups to develop strength in their stomachs. Parallel bar dips and the push-ups Lori is doing below, develop arm strength.

TUMBLING BASICS

The handstand is one of the most important skills in gymnastics. Mark (in the photograph at left) is doing a handstand in his parallel bars routine. In a handstand, the hands, not the feet, are the sole support of the gymnast's body. The handstand position is a part of every boys' and girls' event. As Lori's handstand (in the photograph at right) shows, the gymnast's body should form an absolutely straight line. In the past, gymnasts didn't pay much attention to proper body line and did handstands with an arched, or banana, back. Allowing the back to curve is considered poor and inefficient technique by modern judges.

The first gymnastics move many children learn—often in their own backyards—is called a **roll.** Rolls can be performed both forward and backward. Once the basic rolls are mastered, variations can be added.

Notice how Cathy is changing her body from a stretched position to a

small ball-like position—in other words, a tuck. She rolls on her rounded back as her legs lift up and over her head.

Once the roll is completed, Cathy stands up in the finished position with arms extended. Rolls can also be performed on the balance beam.

Not only can gymnasts tumble forward and backward, they can also tumble sideways. Many people have experienced the joy of doing a **cartwheel,** even without a lesson!

Sara starts from a stand, kicks her lead leg, and then lunges forward and rotates sideways from her hip joint until her lead hand contacts the mat. Then she kicks her legs into the air,

her straight one first, into a straddle position. Her legs remain straight throughout the move. When she's upside down, Sara's body looks like the spokes of a wheel. Her finish looks just like the beginning.

A cartwheel can be performed on one arm or even without touching the floor. A cartwheel without using hands is called an aerial cartwheel.

LEFT OR RIGHT?

If you're learning to do a cartwheel for the first time, how do you know which hand to put down first—your right or your left? When people write, they are naturally either right- or left-handed. In the same way, people usually are right- or left-side tumblers. However, you may write with your right hand but find you prefer to do cartwheels with your left hand first!

Coaches will often encourage gymnasts to learn the basic skills on both sides. When skills are done in combination, it might be easier for the gymnast to have the option of tumbling left or right. Once a gymnast has a preferred side, it's often hard for that person to change.

The **roundoff** is the main maneuver that leads to most backward tumbling combinations. Doing a roundoff correctly is very important for becoming a strong, dynamic backward tumbler.

The roundoff transfers a gymnast's forward power into backward power. It is a change-of-direction skill.

Lori begins her roundoff with a quick run into a **hurdle** or hop step.

Then, she reaches through the **lunge** position and puts down both hands simultaneously.

As she pushes off with her arms, she brings her feet together. When she is upside down, her body rotates over the top so that when she snaps down, she is facing the opposite direction from where she began her roundoff.

You can perform a handspring going backward or forward. The **back handspring** that Beth is doing on this page and the next is sometimes called a flip-flop or a flick-flack.

Beth starts in a stretched, standing

position. She pushes off from her feet and leans backward. She lands on her hands, flips her feet over her head, and then lands on her feet again. She must use explosive power to boost her body high into the air.

FORWARD OR BACKWARD?

Many coaches teach a back handspring and a back somersault before the front versions. It's easier to land a backward skill than it is a forward skill because you can see your hands or your feet land. The landing of a forward move is called a blind landing because you cannot see your feet land before you are there. Think about landing on a 4-inch-wide balance beam!

People sometimes call a **somersault** a "flip." Somersaults are fun to do because as you rotate in the air, for a moment, you feel as if you're flying.

A somersault requires good spatial awareness, which means knowing where you are in the air at all times. A somersault can be done backward, forward, or to the side.

A gymnast often will perform a roundoff or a back handspring in a floor exercise routine just before a somersault.

But somersaults aren't used only in floor exercise routines. A somersault can be done as part of a dismount, which is the skill done when leaving an apparatus.

On these two pages, Pat demonstrates a front somersault. He starts in a stretched position for the takeoff, lifts his arms, and reaches with an explosive thrust. As his arms rise, he pushes off with both feet up into the air. At the top of the lift, Pat is in a tuck, similar to that for a forward roll. His body will then rotate all the way around and he lands on his feet. His hands never touch the floor.

Whether you choose to do a front or back somersault, you can add variations. Your body can be tucked, piked, or in the layout position. If you are in the layout position, you can add a half, full, double-full, or even a triple-full twist.

THE DANCE COMPONENT

Music and dance are a big part of girls' floor exercise routines. Dance is also an element of the balance beam event. In both events, the gymnast must do turns, jumps, and leaps. She should also include runs, walks, and skips, which connect the tumbling and the dance. Gymnasts spend almost as much time and effort learning dance skills as they do learning tumbling skills.

Dance movements in the floor exercise event must be done in harmony with the music and should fit the style of the gymnast. The moves may come from ballet, modern, ethnic, folk, or jazz dance. Whichever style the gymnast chooses, the dance used in gymnastics routines must show good form and flow smoothly.

The friction of the surface of the balance beam or the floor mat makes turning difficult. Gymnasts should perform all turns on the toes and balls of their feet. A gymnast must learn to focus so that she lands the turn where she intended to stop.

A **pivot turn** is the most basic turn. It's a simple turn done with both feet up on their toes. Cathy starts facing one direction and, when finished, faces the opposite direction.

47

48

A **full turn** is required in floor exercise and balance beam routines. Kristy holds her arms up and steps forward onto the ball of one foot. Her free leg may be in any position.

The closer Kristy's leg is to her body, the faster she will turn. She looks straight ahead and turns on her base leg a full 360 degrees so that she faces the same way as when she started.

A jump is a skill in which the gymnast leaves the floor from both feet and then lands on both feet simultaneously.

While she is in the air, the gymnast's legs may be in many different positions. Some examples are illustrated by Sara's straddle jump, above, and Kristy's tuck jump, left.

Leaps are usually performed after a short run to make them dynamic. To execute a leap, a gymnast transfers her weight from one foot to the other as high as possible in the air. Several leaps are often done, one right after the other, to make a series.

Good leaping requires excellent leg strength and flexibility. The **split leap** Jill is doing is the most basic of all the leaps, but still is very challenging. The gymnast's legs should be parallel with the floor and absolutely straight at the height of the leap.

TYPICAL WORKOUT

Gymnasts learn new skills, and create and practice their routines during their workout sessions. Workouts vary depending upon whether they take place before, during, or after the competitive season. Most workouts consist of three parts: warmup, rotations on apparatus, and conditioning.

No coach can overemphasize the importance of warming up properly. During a warmup session, gymnasts stretch, flex, and limber up their entire bodies. Correct techniques are required. These techniques will transfer to the skills the gymnasts perform later in the workout. A warmup usually takes place on the floor mat, but sometimes gymnasts will use the equipment or their teammates.

After the warmup, gymnasts divide into smaller groups to work on the apparatus. The time that a gymnast spends at each event is called a rotation. Most people suggest that no more than six to eight gymnasts work with a coach while on an apparatus. This ratio ensures adequate supervision and assistance for each athlete.

The gymnasts go to different events for set periods of time during the workout. Most coaches agree that even if a gymnast doesn't compete in an event, he or she should work out regularly on each apparatus. Some of the skills that are used for one event are also used in others.

Finally, after the day's rotations are completed, there is time for conditioning. During this time, gymnasts do push-ups, sit-ups, splits, and sprints to increase the strength, flexibility, and endurance they need to execute skills or to learn new ones.

SHOWTIME

Jill is waiting for the green flag. In front of her awaits her biggest challenge of the day—the balance beam. In a few seconds, she will be up on that 4-inch beam that is taller than she is. Soon she will be flipping, turning, dancing, and leaping. And, above all, Jill will be hoping she has prepared well so she will not fall.

Her coach whispers one last thought in her ear, "Do what you know you can do, Jill. You can do it!" The judge raises the green flag. Jill lifts her arms to **salute** the judge. And she's on!

For a minute and a half, Jill is on top of that little piece of wood that is her skinny stage. Let's find out how you can get involved in competitive gymnastics too.

WHAT DOES A COACH DO?

Coaches teach many skills for each type of apparatus. They physically assist or spot all the moves their gymnasts want to learn on all the events. A coach should have a safety certification for gymnastics and should also be trained in first aid.

A coach needs to know about the mental and emotional aspects of gymnastics, too. For example, how can a coach help a gymnast who fears doing a skill? The coach and gymnast must be partners who trust one another.

Gymnasts start competing when they are young. As gymnasts grow and mature, their bodies change and that affects their ability to compete. Most women are done with competitive gymnastics by the time they are 20 years old. Men often continue into their mid-20s. Perhaps this is why many former gymnasts become coaches.

GETTING STARTED IN COMPETION

Community recreation programs and YMCAs often have gymnastics classes but most people who want to be gymnasts join gymnastics clubs. Clubs give gymnasts the chance to compete against athletes from other clubs.

Competitive opportunities are available at many different levels in the United States. If your goal is to be in the Olympics someday, you will want to compete in meets organized by USA Gymnastics (USAG) at the local, state, regional, and national levels. USAG sets the requirements for competition that all member gymnasts and coaches must follow.

The USAG program is organized into levels. The lowest levels are non-competitive and achievement oriented. Competition begins in the middle levels when gymnasts learn compulsory routines that every gymnast must perform in competition.

In the advanced levels, gymnasts create their own routines. These optional routines must include some of the specific skills that are defined in the Code of Points, which are set by the **International Gymnastics Federation.**

Gymnasts compete against other gymnasts at the same level and in the same age group. To move up levels, gymnasts must demonstrate they

have mastered specific skills. The gymnasts you see on television in the Olympics or at other international meets have gone beyond these levels. These competitors are called elite gymnasts.

Some gymnastics clubs compete against each other outside of the USAG system. These independent clubs usually do not follow the USAG rules as strictly as USAG-sponsored programs.

Competition is also available at many junior and senior high schools. Sometimes gymnasts who started competing in a private club decide to join their school's gymnastics team. In this way, they can share the excitement of competition with their friends and represent their schools, too. The schools (and independent clubs) use the National Federation of High School Gymnastics rulebook instead of the Code of Points for their competitions.

Many colleges across the nation have gymnastics teams. Some colleges even provide scholarships for athletes to compete in gymnastics while attending college. College gymnasts usually have experience in high school or private club competition.

GETTING READY FOR A MEET

In USAG competitions, a gymnast must compete in every event. When a gymnast does this, he or she is called an *all-arounder*. For most school and independent club competition, competing all-around is not required. When a gymnast chooses to compete in just one or a few events, he or she is called a *specialist*.

Once the gymnast learns the basic skills, those must be combined into a series of moves. In compulsory competition, these series or combinations are set. In optional competition, the combinations are unique to each gymnast. The gymnast and his or her coach decide on the skills and combinations from the Code of Points that best suit that gymnast's ability and style. The routines must be polished.

For the floor exercise event, the gymnast must have plenty of endurance. The routine should look as easy to perform at the end as it did at the beginning when the gymnast was full of energy. Both the floor exercise and balance beam events are timed, so gymnasts in these events must also practice their timing so that they don't perform their routine too quickly or too slowly.

JUDGING

During a meet, each team is allowed to have a certain number of competitors in each event. Usually, two judges evaluate each routine in each event. For important competitions, there are sometimes as many as four judges.

The judges are looking for a performance that is as close to perfection as possible. Each routine is judged on a 10.0 scale. No matter what level of competition, all routines are worth 10 points if performed perfectly. Points or tenths of a point are deducted for mistakes. The 10 possible points are awarded based on difficulty of the skills (both required and optional), the composition of the routine, and the execution of the skills. Judges give bonus points to gymnasts who perform difficult maneuvers that weren't required in the routine.

Judges follow the rulebook but some of what the judge decides is based on his or her opinion. Judges confer when they don't agree. When the routine is scored by more than one judge, the final score is the average of the judges' scores.

MENTAL PREPARATION

The gymnast also prepares psychologically for competition. When you watch gymnastics, you may wonder, "How does she do that?" and "Won't he get hurt?" A gymnast often fears that he or she may be injured while performing. Overcoming the fear of getting hurt is often as important as learning the skills.

Coaches spot gymnasts while they do maneuvers until the coach is confident that there is very little chance that the gymnast will get hurt. And, coaches don't let a gymnast perform a skill in competition unless the gymnast has first practiced it many, many times. People will sometimes say, "Practice makes perfect," but gymnastics coaches say that, "Perfect practice makes perfect."

When a gymnast is nervous, he or she is more likely to make mistakes that can lead to an injury. Gymnastics is often thought of as an individual sport, but competition also takes place between teams. There is pressure to perform well for teammates and fans. A gymnast might feel that a fall would cost his or her team a victory. Gymnasts must deal with the fear or pressure they may feel.

Many coaches ask their gymnasts to visualize, or imagine, doing their routines perfectly before they go to sleep or right before they compete. Some gymnasts keep a journal or training notebook to record their individual progress, problems, frustrations, and accomplishments. Their coaches read these notebooks and talk with the gymnasts about how to improve their performance and handle their frustrations.

There's no doubt about it—gymnastics is as much a mental as a physical sport.

SAFETY FIRST

Coaches have a responsibility to provide a safe environment in which to learn gymnastics. All equipment should be as up-to-date as possible and it must be checked and rechecked so there is little risk. There should be ample room in between pieces of equipment and enough protective matting for the falls that occur during the learning process. A coach must have the knowledge, technique, and physical ability to teach and spot all skills.

RAZZLE DAZZLE

The goal of many gymnasts is to compete for a gymnastics team and, perhaps, one day to participate in the Olympic Games. To do that, gymnasts must train for many years, avoid injuries as much as possible, and learn advanced skills. Advanced moves come in handy once gymnasts begin to create their own optional routines.

Even if you don't plan on competing in the Olympics, you might enjoy learning new and more difficult maneuvers. Ask your coach for help in learning these skills and remember to always have a spotter when you are working on a new move.

Shannon Miller led the U.S. team to a gold medal in the 1996 Olympics and won an individual gold in the balance beam competition.

For floor exercise routines, gymnasts must learn to do somersaults, such as the back somersault Stacy is performing. Once a gymnast can do front and back flips in the tuck position, he or she can add variations.

Beth shows one such variation as she straightens and splits her legs in this **layout stepout** back flip.

In vaulting, advanced work requires adding twists or somersaults in the postflight. One popular advanced vault is a tsukahara, which is a quarter or half turn onto the horse followed by a back somersault. The vault may be done in the tuck, pike or layout position, with or without adding twists.

Advanced skills on the boys' high bar and girls' uneven parallel bars usually include letting go of the bar in mid-air and then re-grasping it. One such move is Sara's counter, below.

The parallel bars event is unique to boys' gymnastics. Pat is demonstrating a stütz. Pat swings through the bars and releases both hands. He then twists and grabs the bars—and is facing the opposite way from the direction he was originally facing.

Jill demonstrates superb control and flexibility when she performs her needle scale on the balance beam. Gymnasts performing on the rings also use those qualities in many of their advanced moves.

Tony's **scissors** work on the pommel horse requires as much delicacy and accuracy as the back handspring on the beam that Kristy uses (on the next page) to lead into her dismount off the beam.

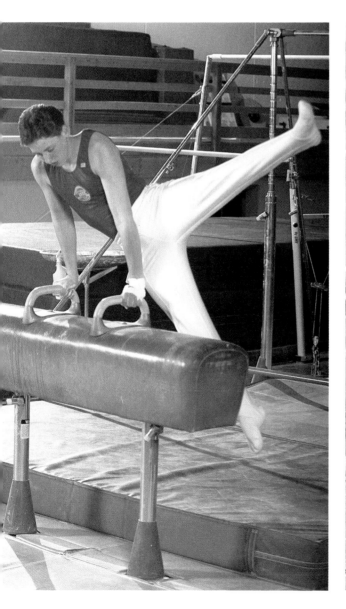

For her dismount off the beam, Kristy jumps backward onto her hands in a back handspring. As she lands back on her feet, Kristy imme-

diately pushes off again. Her momentum gives her extra height as she tucks into a back somersault dismount. She sticks the landing.

Rhythmic gymnasts use balls, ribbons, and hoops to create special effects.

GYMNASTIC COUSINS

The events described in this book are called artistic gymnastics. Rhythmic gymnastics, acrogymnastics, and sports acrobatics are variations of gymnastics.

Only girls and women compete in the Olympic sport of rhythmic gymnastics. Rhythmic gymnastics emphasizes grace, coordination, control, and poise. Gymnasts perform floor exercise routines that include using a ribbon, ball, hoop, club, or rope. The gymnasts perform leaps, jumps, turns, steps, and other dance moves.

Acrogymnastics events include trampoline, double mini-trampoline, synchronized trampoline, and power tumbling.

In sports acrobatics, groups of gymnasts perform routines of tumbling and balancing moves. The performers balance on and somersault from their partners.

Gymnastics is a complex sport in which athletes strive for perfection while trying to make their effort look as easy as possible. It is a sport that constantly changes, continually challenges, and will always be breathtaking to watch at any level.

GYMNASTICS TALK

apparatus: The equipment used in the gymnastics events, specifically: uneven parallel bars, horizontal bar, rings, pommel horse, vault, parallel bars, and balance beam.

back handspring: A jump backward onto the hands, followed by a quick push from the hands to the feet.

balance beam: A wooden or aluminum beam, 4 inches wide, 16 feet, 5 inches long, raised on metal supports 3 feet, 11 inches high.

block: The motion during which a gymnast changes from vertical to horizontal movement by preventing his or her shoulders from moving forward when in a hand support position or by preventing the hips from moving forward in the lunge position.

cartwheel: A rotation of the gymnast's body sideways through the upside down position on the hands and onto the feet, landing one foot at a time with straight legs.

circles: A circular movement of one or both legs on the pommel horse.

comaneci: A dismount from the uneven parallel bars performed by doing a circle off the top bar followed by a quarter twist and back flip.

dismount: A means of leaving the apparatus at the completion of a routine.

floor exercise: A timed gymnastics event performed on a mat measuring 40 feet by 40 feet. Boys perform tumbling skills. Girls perform tumbling and dance skills to music.

front handspring: A forward jump onto the gymnast's hands with immediate rotation forward onto his or her feet.

front walkover: A movement rotating forward round the shoulder axis, with momentary hand support in the upside down position.

full turn: A rotation about the vertical plane of the body in dance. In tumbling, a rotation about the horizontal axis.

giant swing: A skill used on the high bar and uneven parallel bars where the fully extended body circles around the bar.

grips: Devices gymnasts wear on their hands to hold onto the apparatus better. Also called handguards.

handstand: A move in which the gymnast supports his or her body on his or her hands while upside down.

horizontal bar: A metal bar supported by metal poles on which boys perform routines. Also called a high bar.

hurdle: A hop step used to begin a tumbling skill.

International Gymnastics Federation: The governing body of international gymnastics. Also known as FIG after its French translation.

layout: The basic body position in which the gymnast's body is completely stretched out and extended.

layout stepout: A back somersault with the gymnast's legs split and extended.

lunge: A leaning-over position with one foot ahead of the other and the gymnast's weight mainly on his or her lead leg, which is bent.

mount: A method of getting onto the apparatus to start a routine.

pancake: A body position in which the gymnast's upper body is piked over flat to his or her lower body.

parallel bars: A pair of wooden or fiberglass bars of the same height and parallel to each other which are supported by adjustable metal poles. Also called P-bars.

pike: A basic body position in which the gymnast's body is folded at the hips. The gymnast's arms and legs are held straight.

pivot turn: A half-turn on the balls of both feet.

pommel horse: A leather-covered wooden frame with a straight body and two handles, called pommels, screwed into it. Also called a side horse.

postflight: A phase of the vault during which the gymnast's body is in space, from the time the gymnast's hands leave the horse until his or her feet land on the mat.

preflight: A phase of the vault during which the gymnast's body is in space, from the time his or her feet leave the board until the gymnast's hands touch the horse.

rings: A pair of stationary rings supported from ropes and straps. Also called still rings.

roundoff: A cartwheel variation in which the gymnast lands on both feet at the same time, facing the way he or she began.

salute: An arm signal by a gymnast to a judge that indicates that the gymnast is ready to begin his or her routine.

scissors: A move used on the pommel horse in which the legs extend and cross each other.

somersault: A 360-degree rotation of the gymnast's body about its horizontal axis with upward flight and without hand support. Also called a flip or salto or somi.

split leap: A dance skill in which the gymnast pushes off of one foot and transfers her weight from one leg to the other with both legs parallel to the floor at the height of the leap.

spring floor: A type of floor exercise mat made with springs or foam blocks, wooden boards, a foam pad, and carpeting.

stick: The action of landing a dismount without taking a step or completing a beam routine without any falls.

straddle: A body position of straight legs held apart with a wide angle between them.

tsukahara: A type of vault in which the gymnast does a quarter or half twist onto the horse followed by a one and a-half back flip off.

Nikki demonstrates a scale on the balance beam. This pose requires balance and control. Beam routines must show both qualities.

roll: A tucked position moving either forward or backward during which the gymnast starts and ends on his or her feet.

tuck: The basic body position in which the gymnast's knees are bent up to his or her chest, which is rounded, and the gymnast's chin is in and down.

tumbling pass: A series of tumbling skills on the floor exercise event.

twist: To rotate about the body's vertical axis.

uneven parallel bars: A pair of wooden or fiberglass bars on metal supports. The bars are parallel to each other but one is higher than the other. Also called asymmetric bars.

uprights: The vertical poles that support the parallel and uneven parallel bars.

vault: A flat-surfaced, leather-covered rectangular structure on wooden supports. Also called a horse.

V-ups: A sit-up-like movement done with straight legs to strengthen the gymnast's abdominal muscles.

FURTHER READING

Conner, Bart. *Winning the Gold*. New York: Warner Books, Inc., 1985.

Feeney, Rik. *Gymnastics: A Guide for Parents and Athletes*. Indianapolis, Ind.: Masters Press, 1992.

Low, Trevor. *Gymnastics: Floor, Vault, Beam, and Bar*. England: Crowood Press, 1993.

Whitlock, Steve. *Make the Team: Gymnastics for Girls*. Boston, Mass.: The Time Inc. Magazine Company (Little, Brown and Company), 1991.

FOR FURTHER INFORMATION

International Gymnast Magazine
P. O. Box 721020
Norman, OK 73070
www.intlgymnast.com

International Gymnastics Hall of Fame
120 North Robinson
Oklahoma City, OK 73102

USA Gymnastics
201 S. Capital Suite 300
Pan Am Plaza
Indianapolis, IN 46225
www.usa-gymnastics.org

INDEX